"The Sphinx & The Lost Hall of Records" Lecture

John Bunker
and Karen Pressler

Edgar Cayce's A.R.E. Houston Center

"THE SPHINX AND THE LOST HALL OF RECORDS"
Lecture given at the Houston A.R.E. Center
January 17, 2015

Written and presented by
John M. Bunker & Karen L. Pressler

For additional information about the ideas presented in this book
See the companion volume:

Edgar Cayce and the Hall of Records
©2014

"Ask, and it shall be given you;
Seek, and ye shall find;
Knock, and it shall be opened unto you"

Jesus Christ
(King James Bible)

Index

Acknowledgements

We would like to extend our appreciation to the Edgar Cayce A.R.E. Houston Center, our gracious hosts for the lecture we are reproducing in this book. Their staff and members were most helpful and lovely.

Thank you to Bob Charles and the Pyramid One International radio network, who extended our live audience to 108 countries around the world!

And thanks to Ben Breman, our excellent son-in-law, cameraman, and technician for the lecture. He was responsible for all of the arrangements on site that allowed us to connect with the internet radio broadcast.

***Thanks to all the supportive and helpful
family, friends, and individuals
who have been a part this project along the way.***

Preface

This lecture was given to explain the reasons behind the theory that the Egyptian Hall of Records lies *at the top of the middle pyramid (Khafre's) at Gizeh.* We have studied astronomy and learned to translate hieroglyphs in order to answer our own questions about the validity of Edgar Cayce's psychic readings regarding the Hall of Records and the history of the human race. This has led us to some fascinating conclusions that we enjoy sharing with people who aren't afraid to consider alternatives to what has been "thought" before, and has become accepted as "fact," mainly because nobody questions it. We believe there's much more to it than those original ideas allow.

Many individuals and organizations have searched for decades for this illusive storehouse of information and artifacts from a prehistoric time - one that predates anything we currently know. It's potential to unify the diverse cultures of our planet with a common history makes it worthy of our attention.

If simple testing were done to confirm the validity
of the location suggested here,
we could be very close to opening the greatest treasure of all –
one that may change everything we think we know
about ourselves and each other.

The following is our PowerPoint presentation and lecture. Each slide should be considered with the discussion following it.

[NOTE: For a more detailed and thorough examination of these ideas and more, see the companion book *Edgar Cayce and the Hall of Records.*]

Am Tuat

Seshu	natu	ament	aha	bau	neteru	khaib-t	khu	aru
writings	paintings	hidden	positions	souls	gods	shadows	spirits	forms

Writings & paintings of the hidden positions of souls, gods, shadows, spirits, forms

hat	upt	ament	sba	en	akhet	ament	peh	smau-keku
beginning	daily task	hidden	star	of	horizon	hidden	end	utter darkness

beginning daily, the hidden star of the hidden horizon ends the utter darkness,

sba	akhet	amentt
star	horizon	abode of the dead

the star of the horizon of the abode of the dead

The Clues

The Egyptians wrote about the stars in a book we call *Am Tuat* (or *Amduat*). The book itself claims to be *The Book of Praises of the Other World Above.* There have been translations done of the *Am Tuat,* but so far none have considered that the science of astronomy was central in the lives of the ancient Egyptians and their forebears.

The first slide shows how the Book of Am Tuat begins.

In Egyptian it says:
> *Seshu natu ament aha ba neteru khaib-t khu aru hat upt*
> *ament sba en akhut ament peh sma-u-keku sba akhut amentet*

In English it means:
> *The writings and paintings of the hidden positions of souls, gods, shadows, spirits, forms beginning daily, the hidden star of the hidden horizon ends the utter darkness, the star of the horizon of the abode of the dead.*

This sentence is likely referring to star constellations and their nightly appearing and disappearing.

It began in Chicago in the Spring of 1994 …

THIS IS THE TRUE STORY OF
OUR DISCOVERY OF THE HALL OF RECORDS

Edgar Cayce

It began in Chicago in the spring of 1994. We were in a used bookstore with our friend Matthew Block and we purchased a book titled *The Story of Edgar Cayce, There is a River*, by Thomas Sugrue, and so we became acquainted with Edgar Cayce.

In 1994 we got Edgar Cayce Readings on CD

THE
COMPLETE
EDGAR CAYCE
READINGS

We learned that Cayce was once a high priest in ancient Egypt

In December 1994, I received The Complete Edgar Cayce Readings on CD ROM as a gift from Karen. Thereafter, I studied the Cayce readings at every opportunity! I learned that Cayce experienced an incarnation in ancient Egypt as a High Priest at the beginning of the Egyptian civilization in remote antiquity.

There were many readings about the Sphinx and the great pyramids. I found myself seeking other sources of historical information about ancient Egypt and I purchased many books on that subject. There was so much to learn!

Sphinx = Mystery

= the Egyptian word …

Sheta

This is how they wrote Sphinx.

The Egyptian Texts

In the readings, Cayce referred to the Sphinx as 'the Mystery.' This led us to discover the ancient Egyptian word *sheta*, which means Mystery. After that, we began to learn the picture symbols that the ancient Egyptians used to write their language. This was the beginning of our education of reading and writing ancient Egyptian hieroglyphs.

[NOTE: We have been criticized for our use of Budge in the bulk of our translations, but we are unable to find any genuine reasons for the current popular rejection of his work. Rather, we have found it to be the most comprehensive original compilation of Old Kingdom hieroglyphics available today. We have also focused more on the recurring themes that appear throughout the ancient texts, rather than specific rules of grammar that the scholars have agreed upon. No one knows exactly how the ancient sentence structure was arranged, but if you can step away from that and see the broader meanings they were trying to convey, there is much to be learned, regardless of sentence structure.]

So ...

We practiced writing hieroglyphs

We studied the Cayce readings

We wrote our first book in 1999

EDGAR CAYCE
AND
THE URANTIA BOOK

Edgar Cayce   Dr. William Sadler

JOHN BUNKER
KAREN PRESSLER

I spent many months filling the pages of spiral notebooks with images of hieroglyphs, writing them over and over, learning the Egyptian alphabet. During those first five years, we made many trips to Chicago to visit used bookstores to find more books about Edgar Cayce. In fact, we learned so much about Cayce that we wrote our first book about him and published it in 1999, *Edgar Cayce and the Urantia Book.*

About the same time ….

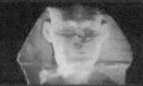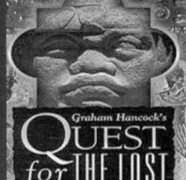

During those years Graham Hancock and Robert Bauval released their books: *The Message of the Sphinx* and *The Secret Chamber.*

Graham Hancock is also known for his television documentary series "Quest for the Lost Civilization." During one of the episodes, on his laptop computer he used the shareware program Sky Globe, with which the positions of stars could be viewed as they were in ancient times.

Skyglobe Astronomical Software Program

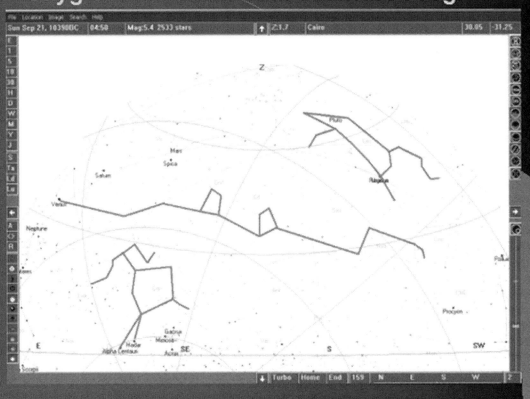

Astronomy

We located this same computer shareware program on the Internet, downloaded it, and learned to use it.

Over the next 15 years, we immersed ourselves into the study of the Edgar Cayce readings, astronomy, and ancient Egyptian texts.

Cayce said, 'Yet as time draws nigh when changes are to come about, there may be the opening of those **three places** where the **records are one**, to those that are the initiates in the knowledge of the One God.'

In this reading, Cayce spoke of

the three places where the records are one.

What were these three places and how could they be opened?

What was the knowledge of the One God?

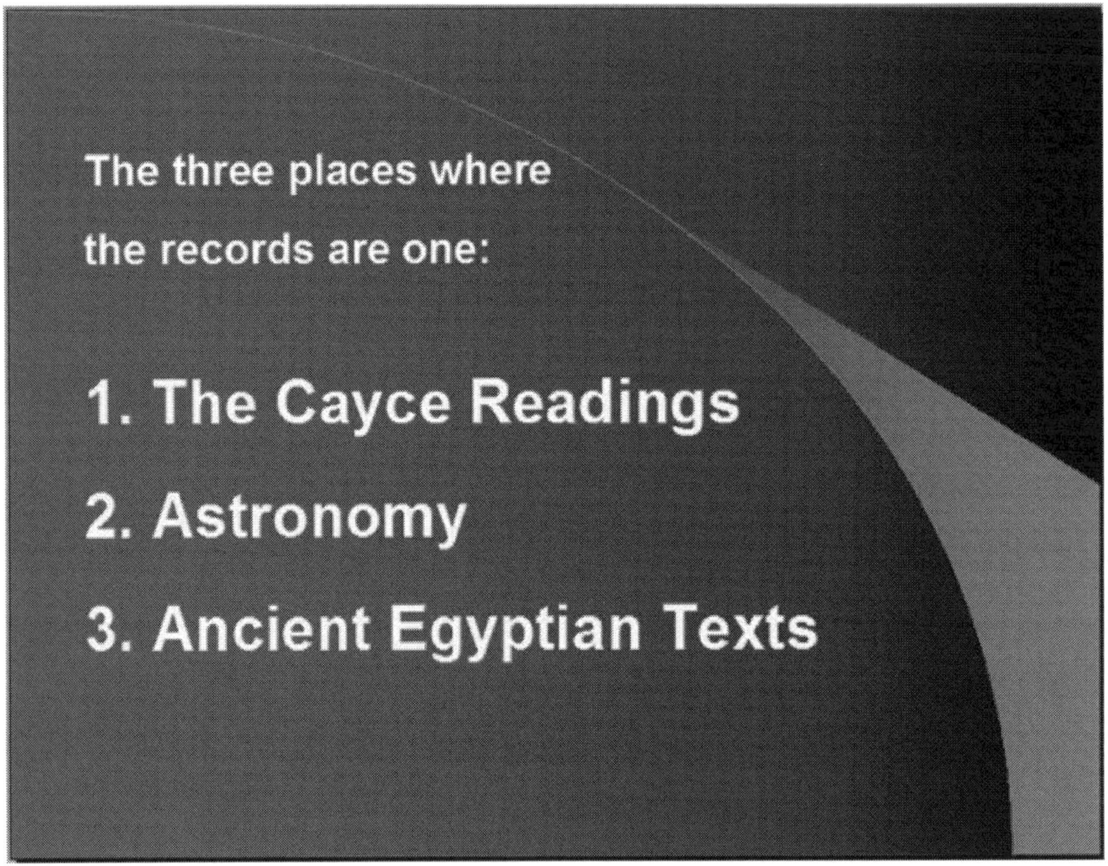
The three places where
the records are one:
1. The Cayce Readings
2. Astronomy
3. Ancient Egyptian Texts

Could the three places referred to by the readings be the readings themselves, astronomy, and ancient Egyptian texts?

Until now, no one had combined the study of these three topics.

Almost everyone in this day and age has heard of the Sphinx and the great pyramids in Egypt. Many people have also heard of Edgar Cayce, but few people have studied the Edgar Cayce material very closely. For this reason, the misinterpretation was made that a tunnel from the right paw of the Sphinx leads to the Hall of Records.

This idea has been popularized, and there have been efforts made to find an underground tunnel near the paw of the Great Sphinx.

Here is what Cayce actually said:

'When there was the entrance of Araart and Araaraart, they began to build upon those mounds that were discovered through research. With the storehouse or record house (where the records are still to be uncovered), there is a chamber or **passage from the right forepaw to this entrance of the record chamber**, *or record tomb. This may not be entered without an understanding, for those that were left as guards may NOT be passed until after a period of their regeneration in the Mount, or the fifth root race begins.'* (5748-6, #17)

At some time, someone read the facing paragraph from an Edgar Cayce reading and saw the phrase *'passage from the right forepaw to this entrance of the record chamber'* and concluded that there was a tunnel from the paw of the monument of the Great Sphinx to the Hall of Records. The rest of the paragraph was ignored, because no one could understand it. That is why even unto this day, people continue to look for the Hall of Records under the Sphinx, but it may never be found there!

We will explain alternative ideas that seem to have much more validity, and would not be difficult to investigate.

Gaston Maspero French
Egyptologist (1846-1916)

"Even in Maspero's day, subterranean chambers were imagined to lie underneath the Sphinx. Not until the last decades of the twentieth century did electromagnetic resistivity testing on the surfaces of the statue put an end to these allegations."

Christiane Zivie-Coche, in her book *Sphinx: History of a Monument*, says,

> "... even in Maspero's day, subterranean chambers were imagined to lie underneath the Sphinx. Not until the last decades of the twentieth century did electromagnetic resistivity testing on the surfaces of the statue put an end to these allegations."

Even today, no one has turned their attention from the idea of an underground chamber.

The Real Location of the Hall of Records

Today we will compare:

-the readings of Edgar Cayce

-ancient texts from the Valley of the Kings

-astronomy

During this presentation, we will provide information from three places that support a single idea:

The location of Edgar Cayce's Hall of Records is inside the top of one of the Gizeh pyramids, not underground.

We will look closely at Cayce's readings and compare them with information from ancient Egyptian texts found in the tombs of the Valley of the Kings of Egypt. We will also compare these ideas with astronomy. When we do this, an entirely new idea develops about the location of the Hall of Records.

You must have all three pieces of the puzzle
to see the whole picture.

In reading 5748-6 Cayce said:

'*This may not be entered without an understanding, for those that were left as guards may NOT be passed until after a period of their regeneration in the Mount,* **or the fifth root race begins.'**
(5748-6, #17)

The readings cause us to ask:

<u>When will the Fifth Root Race begin?</u>

When will the Fifth Root Race begin?

The same reading explains that:

'... *the beginning of a new sub-race, or a change, which - as indicated from the astronomical or numerical conditions - dates from the* **later portion or the middle portion of the present fall [1932]** *... there will be the beginning of the change in the races ... the changes as indicated and outlined are for the* **latter part of the present year [1932].**' (5748-6)

The First Condition

Earlier in this same reading, (5748-6) Cayce explained that *'the beginning of a new sub-race, or a change, which - as indicated from the astronomical or numerical conditions - dates from the later portions or the middle portion of the present fall [1932] ... there will be the beginning of the change in the races...the changes as indicated and outlined are for the present year [1932].'*

Cayce gave this reading in the summer of 1932, and his prediction for the beginning of the Fifth Root Race was, at that time, referring to a future event in the Autumn of that year. That is why the beginning of the Fifth Root Race is presented as a futuristic event. To those present with Cayce at the time of this reading, he *was* predicting a future event. This explains the first of two conditions necessary for the eventual entrance into the Hall of Records.

It was fulfilled in 1932.

We must also attain a <u>specific knowledge</u>.

Cayce said:

'*This* [sealed room] *may not be entered without an understanding, for those that were left as* **guards** *may NOT be passed until after a period of their* **regeneration** *in the* **Mount**.'

The comprehension of this cryptic message was necessary to enter the Hall of Records.

The Second Condition

The second condition is the attainment of a special knowledge.

Understanding this mysterious message is necessary before the Hall of Records may be entered. Let's reason this out together. The guards who were left MAY be passed after they are regenerated in the Mount.

That's what they are telling us in this reading!

That's when the Hall of Records may be entered.

Who were the Guards?

7-1-32 reading:

'those who were left as guards' is **PLURAL**

> Selim Hassan said: "Sphinxes are always found in pairs when guarding temple doorways"

10-29-33 reading:

'the Sphinx that was later set as a sentinel or guard is **SINGULAR**

Who or what were the guards?

Part of this understanding is to recognize that there was more than one guard. On July 1st, 1932, Cayce identified <u>those</u> who were left as guards as a group (in a plural sense). There is no mistaking this!

In his 1949 book, *The Sphinx: Its History in Light of Recent Excavations*, Selim Hassan explains,

"Sphinxes are always found in pairs when guarding temple door-ways."

This will be important to remember as we continue.

More than one year later, on October 29th, 1933, Cayce made another statement about the Sphinx. He identified it as *the Sphinx that was later set as a sentinel or guard*, in a singular sense, <u>and</u> he indicated that it was created at a later date!

So we are talking about different guards!
It is important to see this distinction.

IMPLICATION …

Before the Sphinx was set as a guard, other guards were *already* guarding the Hall of Records!

Who or what were the other guards that guarded the Hall of
Records before the monument of the Sphinx was set as guard?

'In the building of the pyramid, and that which is now called **the Mystery of Mysteries**, this was intended to be a MEMORIAL - as would be termed today - to that counselor who ruled or governed, or who acted in the capacity of the director in the MATERIAL things in the land. With the return of the priest (as it had been stopped), **this was later** - by Isis, the queen, or the daughter of Ra - **turned so as to present** to those peoples in that land the relationships of man and the animal or carnal world with those changes that fade or fall away in their various effect. ... (continued next slide)

Let's recall that within the readings, Cayce referred to the Sphinx as the *Mystery*.

'... These may be seen in a different manner presented in many of the various sphinxes, as called, in other portions of the land - as **the lion with the man**, the various forms of wing, or characterizations in their various developments. These were as presentations of those projections that had been handed down in their various developments of that which becomes man - as in the present.' (5748-6, #17)

That is ....

'the Mystery of Mysteries ...
was later ... turned so as to present ....
the lion with the man'

Reading between the lines, we can see another message ... look at what is concealed in this reading:

> '... *the Mystery of Mysteries was later turned* (changed) *so as to present the lion with the man.'*

It was not always a lion and a man!

This information caused us to study the Sphinx chronology closely.

The Sphinx Chronology

Christiane Zivie-Coche states: *"There are no references to the Sphinx in documents of the Old Kingdom, and during the Middle Kingdom the site of Giza was almost abandoned."*

Mark Lehner also states:

"We are confronted by a complete absence of Old Kingdom texts which mention it."

The Sphinx Chronology

Referring again to the book, *Sphinx: History of a Monument*, Christiane Zivie-Coche states:

"There are no references to the Sphinx in documents of the Old Kingdom, and during the Middle-Kingdom the site of Giza was almost abandoned."

Mark Lehner, Egyptologist and former A.R.E. Member, stated:

"We are confronted by a complete absence of Old Kingdom texts which mention it." [1]

Doesn't it seem like, if the ancient Egyptians built the Sphinx, they would have written something about it? Perhaps the ancient Egyptians of the Old Kingdom did write about the Sphinx ...

... but maybe they called it the Mystery!

That's what the Cayce readings called it.

---

[1] *Cambridge Archaeological Journal*, 1992.

Book of the Dead

Cayce advised, "*Study the Book of the Dead (though this is given as being prepared at a much later date than in reality)*"

ru	sheta	ren	en	pu	ua	sa
lion	mystery	name	of	this	ONE	guard

Lion Mystery is the name of this ONE guard

shetat	bes	sheta	en	khert neter
secret chamber	statue of a god	mystery	of	necropolis

The secret chamber and the sphinx statue of a god of the Necropolis

Cayce advised, *"Study the Book of the Dead (though this is given as being prepared at a much later date than in reality.)"*

What Cayce is telling us here is that the *Book of the Dead* originated at a very, very remote date, so far back that no one knows when it started.

So we searched the original Egyptian hieroglyphic text of the *Book of the Dead*. Since Cayce used *'Mystery'* as another name for the Sphinx, we looked for that word and found these references:

Lion mystery [*sphinx*] **is the name of this ONE guard**

-- from Lepsius *Todtenbuch*, Plate 78

There is the word and there's what it means, and it's real easy to understand!

Here is another one:

The secret chamber and the mystery [*sphinx*] **statue
of a god of the Necropolis**

-- from the Papyrus of Mut-hetep

'...all gathered about that plat builded in the holy city between the facing of what afterward became the sphinx and the holy mount...' (457-2, #11)

The readings explain that originally the head of the Sphinx stood alone as a monument. It was the face of a great councilor who worked for the King of Egypt (Reading 953-24). Centuries later, the body of a lion was sculpted under it by excavation.

Reading 457-2, #11 describes a gathering of people for the sealing of the Hall of Records in the area of land between two landmarks: (1.) *the facing of what afterward became the Sphinx* and (2.) *the holy mount.*

The **plat** referred to in this reading is an area of land, so all the people, in ancient times, gathered between these two structures for the sealing of the Hall of Records.

Below are several statements from the readings that relate to the face of the sphinx:

1. *the facing of what afterward became the Sphinx* (457-2, #11)

2. *the face, even as was given then, is the representation of this councilor* (953-024, #6)

3. *this was later turned…so as to present…the lion with the man* (5748-6, #17)

What was the "facing" of the Sphinx?

These readings indicate that the monument of the face of the Sphinx was created first.

At a later date, the body of a lion was added to it!

[**Arsha** (Ra-Ta period)] *arranged for the restoration of monuments that were being restored and builded in those places, being then the founder of now that mystery of mysteries, the Sphinx.* (195-14, #19)

There was even then the seeking through the channels that are today called archaeological research. (5748-6, #17)

Reading 195-14, #19 explains how the body of the Sphinx was created centuries after the face. It explains there was a man, Arsha, who came into Egypt with the arrival of Araart and his people from the North, who invaded Egypt and took control. This was about 11,000 BC. Arsha lived during the first dynasty of Araart and his son Araaraart.

Monuments were unearthed and added to from time to time. (341-9, #5)

During this initial period, there was the restoration of monuments that were discovered through archaeological research. Monuments were pre-existent at Gizeh <u>before</u> the arrival of the first Egyptian dynasty, the remains of an unknown, vanished ancient civilization. The new settlers excavated these, and that is what the reading is talking about.

Development of the Sphinx Monument took place over centuries

The Sculpting of the face monument

9 YEARS

The deluge of Atlantis and the construction of the Great Pyramid

CENTURIES LATER

Excavation of the body of the Sphinx

Reading 195-14 indicates that the time involved in the development of the monument of the Sphinx took place over *centuries*. Construction of the Great Pyramid was begun about the same time as the deluge of Atlantis. The pyramid was completed in 10,390 BC, at which time there was the sealing of the Hall of Records and all gathered between the facing of what afterward became the Sphinx and the holy mount.

The readings specify that several hundred years passed after the deluge before excavations were made to dig out the base of the Sphinx. This indicates the lion-body was added later, under the monument of the face of the Councilor!

Development of the Sphinx Monument took place over centuries

The Sculpting of the face monument

9 YEARS

The deluge of Atlantis and the construction of the Great Pyramid

CENTURIES LATER

Excavation of the body of the Sphinx

In the lower picture you can see how the rock of the plateau was cut away to create the body of the lion. To accomplish this, channels were laid out and the stone was dug out to create the base (the body). The readings explain that this was in the land above the place where the temple of Isis stood during the days of the deluge (of Atlantis), which occurred centuries before this excavation was begun!

They also explain that the sculpting of the head-monument (which eventually was turned into the Sphinx) happened before the political turmoil involving the priest Ra-Ta. (The readings tell us that Ra-Ta was the first high priest of Egypt, an incarnation of Edgar Cayce!) Because of the resulting chaos, the work on the head-monument (already in progress) had stopped. Ra-Ta was banished to Nubia.

Nine years passed and he returned to Egypt. Thereafter, the great pyramid was built. With the completion of Gizeh, there were ceremonies of dedication and the sealing of the Hall of Records. Centuries later the monument of the councilor was turned into what became known as the Sphinx by excavating the body of a lion under it. This is what is meant by reading 5748-6 that reads: the Sphinx was later set as the sentinel or guard.

This chronology is important to understand.

Recall that the second condition necessary to enter the Hall of Records was the attainment of a special knowledge.

'This may not be entered without an understanding, for those that were left as guards may NOT be passed until after a period of their regeneration in the Mount.'

(5748-6, #17)

We have determined that the second condition necessary to enter the Hall of Records was the attainment of a special knowledge.

Here is how Cayce stated it: *'This may not be entered without an understanding, for those that were left as guards may NOT be passed until after a period of their regeneration in the Mount.'*

But who were these other guards, referred to by Cayce in 1932, over a year before he talked about the Sphinx?

And how can these guards be regenerated?

I have to admit, for many years we were stumped by this.

How could the Guards be Regenerated?

**To regenerate means
to bring into renewed existence
or generate again.**

How are the Guards Regenerated?

By definition, to *regenerate* means to bring into renewed existence or generate again.

Regenerate in what Mount?

Cayce described the Mount in this way:

*'Thou has shown us the pattern **in the mount of our own consciousness**.'*

(254-101, # 22)

To what mount was Cayce referring when he said, the guards' *'regeneration in the Mount.'*?

We searched the readings and discovered reading 254-101, in which he described the Mount.

> *'Thou has shown us the pattern in the mount of our own consciousness.'*

We realized that the Mount is within each of us, and then we understood that the identity of the guards must be realized in our minds! This knowledge of the identity of the guards must have been previously known, but over time it was lost or forgotten.

So what Cayce meant was that
our **recognition** of the guards would
be their **regeneration!**

But who, or what, were the guards?

Earlier in reading 5748-6, Cayce used the phrase, "*As indicated from the astronomical.*" This is an allusion to astronomy, and it suggested to us that there might be a connection between the guards and the stars, because the ancient Egyptians combined astronomy with religion. So we reasoned: if we thought in terms of astronomy, we might have a better chance of understanding their religious ideas.

Papyrus of Ani

In the papyrus of Ani we find:

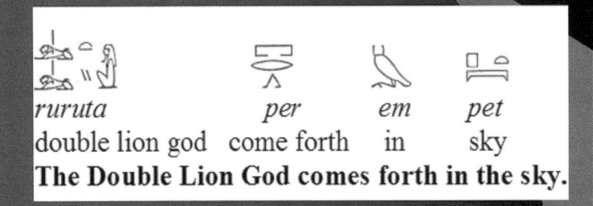

ruruta	*per*	*em*	*pet*
double lion god	come forth	in	sky

The Double Lion God comes forth in the sky.

The papyrus of Ani is the largest, the most perfect, and the best illustrated of all the papyri containing copies of the Theban Recension of the *Book of the Dead*, and was written between 1500 BC and 1350 BC. In the papyrus of Ani we find:

ruruta   *per* *em* *pet*
double lion god come forth in sky
The Double Lion God comes forth in the sky

That seems pretty clear. It has to be talking about constellations!

Tomb Drawings may have Astronomical Connections

Fifth Division of the Am Tuat

This is an image from an ancient Egyptian book painted in the tombs of the Kings of Egypt. In the center is a mysterious oval that rests on the bodies of two sphinxes.

Recall the quote mentioned earlier from Salim Hassan that *"Sphinxes are always found in pairs when guarding temple doorways."* If this is an illustration of the location of the Hall of Records, as we believe it is, then how appropriate that two sphinxes are shown guarding it.

Hieroglyphic text (not shown here) painted in the original tomb describes these sphinxes as the guards. What if this image has some sort of astronomical connection? Since Cayce said the sealing of the Hall of Records was at the completion of Giza in 10,390 BC, we decided to begin looking at the positions of stars during that year.

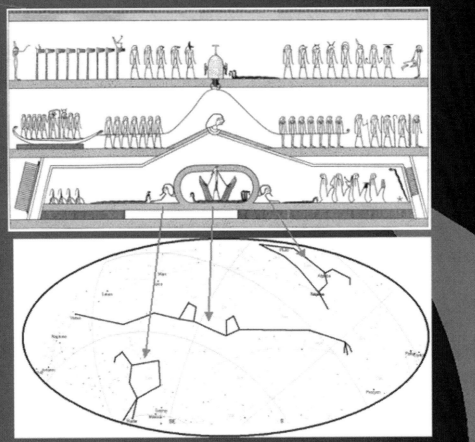

September 21, 10,390 BC at 4:50 AM. over Cairo

Using a computer to recreate the positions of the stars to their same positions in ancient times, we discovered that the two sphinxes in the tomb drawing were in fact star constellations at opposite ends of the horizon, represented in the tomb drawing by an oval. The **oval** is the ancient Egyptian hieroglyph for the word 'horizon.' The **winged serpent** is the constellation Hydra at its zenith (zenith means the highest point in the sky a constellation reaches). The **head of a god** (at the tail of Hydra in the tomb illustration) represents the planet Venus in the sky. This configuration of stars and planets took place over Giza on a specific date, and by using astronomy we can identify the date and time ....

SEPTEMBER 21, 10390 BC AT 4:50 AM
OVER CAIRO
JUST BEFORE SUNRISE

This is a very important date and time to become familiar with in Egyptian history. The ancient kings of Egypt illustrated these star configurations in their tombs for over *300 years*!

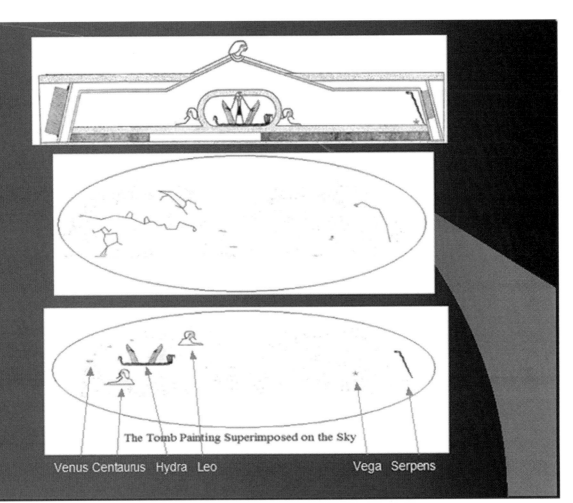

The Tomb Painting Superimposed on the Sky

Venus Centaurus Hydra Leo   Vega Serpens

This illustration shows the whole sky compared with the scene painted in the tomb of Tuthmosis III.

- At the top we have the tomb painting showing the relevant characters.

- In the center, the characters from the painting are shown as their corresponding constellations in the sky

- The lower illustration shows the sky with the figures from the tomb painting superimposed over it. The names of the planets, stars, and constellations are included. **Serpens** is the Latin word for serpent. **Vega** was the brightest star in the sky, and if you looked north - at this time on this date - your attention would be drawn to Vega because it was the brightest thing you could see in the sky. If you turned around and looked behind you, you would see two lion constellations, **Leo** and **Centaurus,** with this big flying serpent, **Hydra** between them. And at the end of the tail of Hydra, at that time on that date, you would see the planet **Venus**.

Cayce said:

*'With the **storehouse** or **record house** (where the records are still to be uncovered), there is a chamber…'*

The Pyramid of Records

Cayce told us that there is a record chamber where the records still exist within the storehouse.

Let's reconsider his words in the context of the language used within the body of the readings …

1. *'Those* **storehouses** *in those pyramids or mounds yet to be uncovered'* (1925-1, #10)

This reading and the one on the following slide identify pyramids as storehouses.

The pyramids were mounds of stone that contained storehouses or storage chambers.

2. *'The entity saw what was preserved as memorials, the pyramids built during the entity's sojourn; when there was begun the pyramid of understanding, or **Gizeh** – and only **to the king's chamber was the pathway built**. The entity's harps - and the entities menus, as they would be termed in the present – are among those things preserved in the pyramid of UNKNOWN ORIGIN, as yet - but in the **storehouse of records**.'* (275-33, #21-22)

This reading actually refers to two Gizeh pyramids:

A. One has a pathway to the King's chamber (Khufu).

B. One is the storehouse of records.

In this reading Cayce is talking about pyramids at Gizeh! They specifically tell us that in this reading. There are three great pyramids at Gizeh.

- o The first pyramid referred to is the Great Pyramid. It can be identified by the mention of the king's chamber.

- o The other pyramid was identified as the Storehouse of Records, which is also the Hall of Records!

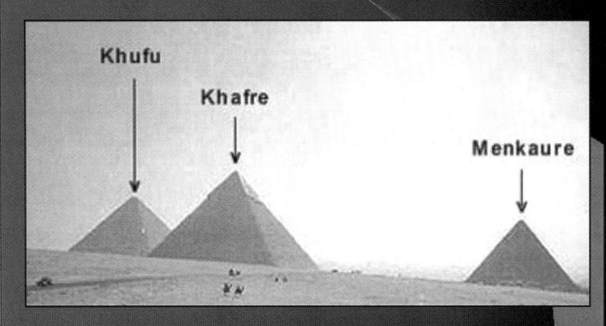

Consider this:

There are only three great pyramids at Gizeh. That means that the Pyramid of Records must be either Khafre's pyramid or Menkaure's pyramid.

But how do we know which one?

Cayce gives us further information about the Hall of Records by identifying it in relationship to its position with the Sphinx causeway.

(Q) Where are those records or tablets made of that Egyptian experience, which I might study?

*(A) In the Tomb of Records, as indicated. For the entity's tomb then was a part of the Hall of Records, which has **not yet been uncovered**. **It lies between - or along that entrance from the Sphinx to the temple - or the pyramid; in a pyramid, of course, of its own**.*

(2329-3, #36)

The Location of the Hall of Records

Cayce gives us further information about the Hall of Records by identifying its position with respect to the Sphinx causeway. Here he is telling us that the Hall of Records is in proximity to the Sphinx, along the causeway from the Sphinx to the pyramid located behind it.

Khafre Pyramid

He is also telling us in the same reading that the pyramid containing the Hall of Records is not yet uncovered, and that the records are in a pyramid of their own.

- o In this picture you can see that the pyramid of Khafre is still covered at the top with the original casing stone, satisfying the condition of *"not yet uncovered"*

- o If the top of the pyramid was built much later than the bottom, as it seems to have been, then the upper portion is a *"pyramid of its own"*

"It lies along that entrance from the Sphinx to the temple - or the pyramid; **in a pyramid, of course, of its own**." (2329-3, # 36)

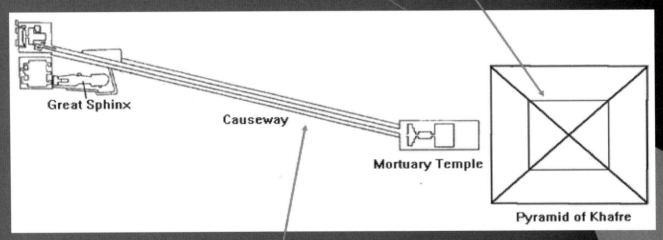

'The chambers of **the way** between the Sphinx and the pyramid of records.' (1486-1, #29) 'The place of records that leadeth from the Sphinx to the Hall of Records in the Egyptian land.' (2012-1, #31)

So here is what Cayce said about the Hall of Records:

o   *It lies along that entrance from the Sphinx to the temple - or the pyramid; in a pyramid, of course, of its own.*

o   *The chambers of the way between the Sphinx and the pyramid of records.*

o   *The place of records that leadeth from the Sphinx to the Hall of Records in the Egyptian land.*

'This in position lies, as the sun rises from the waters, the line of the shadow falls between the paws of the Sphinx, that was later set as the sentinel or guard' (378-16)

'The temples of records that lie just beyond that enigma that still is the mystery of mysteries.' (2402-2)

In describing the location of the Hall of Records, Cayce also said:

'This in position lies, as the sun rises from the waters, ...

[Note: At this time is history the river Nile was much closer to the Gizeh plateau than it is today. Today it is five miles away from the Sphinx. The course of the Nile has moved over the last 12,000 years.]

... the line of the shadow falls between the paws of the Sphinx, that was later[2] set as the sentinel or guard' (Reading 378-16, #11)

LOOK AT WHAT LIES JUST BEYOND THE SPHINX! THERE IS AN ALIGNMENT OF THE SUN WITH THE PAWS OF THE SPHINX AND THE PYRAMID OF KHAFRE!

Cayce called it: *'The temples of records that lie just beyond that Enigma that still is the Mystery of Mysteries.'* (Reading 2402-2, #38)

---

[2] *The Sphinx that was later set as the sentinel or guard'* may indicate there was an earlier sphinx.

'*This in position lies, as the sun rises from the waters, the line of shadow falls between the paws of the Sphinx, that was later set as the sentinel or guard.*

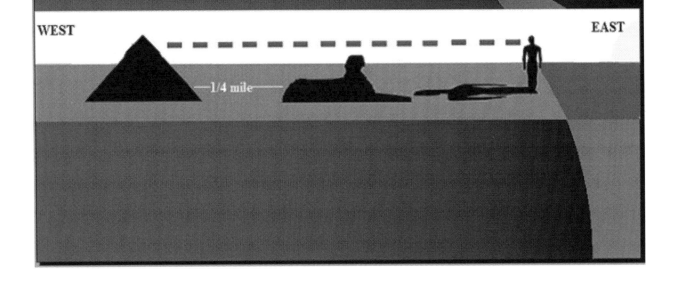

WEST

EAST

—1/4 mile—

The Entrance

The position of the sealed room lies west of the Sphinx monument, which was later set as a sentinel to guard the pyramid of records beyond it. If an observer were standing between the Sphinx and the river, the line of the observer's shadow would fall between the paws of the Sphinx - making an alignment with the pyramid, about ¼ mile away, where the sealed room is located. Our drawing is very condensed, but this ¼ mile area is where all the people gathered for the ceremony of the sealing of the Hall of Records, when there was just the head of the Sphinx and the body had not yet been added.

But what about the idea that the Hall of Records may be entered from the connecting chambers from the Sphinx's right paw? Does this mean there is a tunnel from the paw of the Sphinx to the Hall of Records?

Or could it have another meaning?

'When there was the entrance of Araart and Araaraart, **they begin to build upon those mounds** which were discovered through research. With **the storehouse, or record house** (where the records are still to be uncovered), there is a chamber or passage from the right forepaw to this entrance of the record chamber, or record tomb.'

(5748-6, #7, given on 7/1/32)

Returning to reading 5748-6, the idea is cleverly presented that the storehouse or record house was built *upon a mound*. This will become a significant clue as we explore other possible avenues of inquiry.

To begin, let's look further at the idea of the paw of the sphinx and what this might refer to, in addition to the obvious assumption.

Other Possibilities ...

'These may be seen in a different manner presented in many of the various sphinxes, as called, in other portions of the land.' (5748-6)

Which Sphinx?

Let's explore some other possibilities! Cayce indicated that there were many examples of sphinxes in Egypt, not just one.

If we are dealing with more than one sphinx in connection with the Hall of Records, we need to identify them. To do this we should ask:

Of the various sphinxes in Egypt, and there are many, are there any located in a position with its right paw pointing toward the entrance of a chamber in a pyramid?

The paw of the sphinx points toward a sealed entrance
in this tomb drawing.

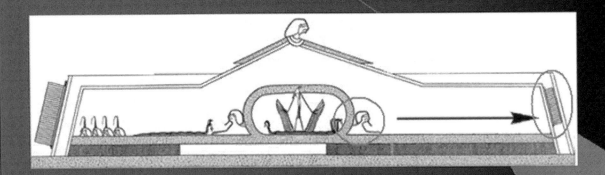

'… *that record for future entering souls will be
physically known when time has set its mark.*'
(378-16, #15)

The answer can be found hidden in the tombs of the Valley of the Kings in Egypt, where there is an illustration of two sphinx guardians in a chamber within the top of a pyramid (you can see the pyramid centered above them) whose right paw points the way to a sealed entrance.

Cayce's phrase, *'that record for future entering souls will be physically known when time has set its mark,'* causes us to ask:

What is the Mark of Time?

What is the Mark of time?
The mark of time is the date!

Venus   Centaurus   Hydra   Leo   Vega   Serpens

September 21, 10,390 BC over Gizeh
4:50 AM

The Mark of Time

Earlier Cayce said the Hall of Records may not be entered until the time had been fulfilled. What exactly does this mean? One synonym for fulfilled is *realized*. So what he may have been saying was that the TIME needed to be *realized*.

The Mark of time is the date!

In this case, the date is the sealing of the Hall of Records: September 21st, 10390 BC, at 4:50 AM over Egypt, just before sunrise.

In our illustration we are showing a 360-degree view of the sky over Egypt, just before sunrise.

This date is known by means of information from three places: astronomy, ancient Egyptian texts, and Edgar Cayce's readings.

Astronomical Dating
agrees with
the Edgar Cayce Readings

When asked for the exact date of the construction of the
Great Pyramid, Cayce said it was begun in 10,490 BC
and completed in 10,390 BC. He further stated at the
completion of Gizeh, there was the sealing of the Hall of
Records, and all the people gathered about for this
record sealing. This was a pretty big event for its day.
When we look at the tombs of the ancient Kings of
Egypt, we find they *consistently* marked the year 10,390
BC, but until now, this had not been recognized.

To see the connection with the astronomy of the ancient
Egyptians, their mythology must be taken into
consideration.

A prominent Egyptian myth told of the daily battle of the Sun god, Ra, against the evil serpent, Apep.

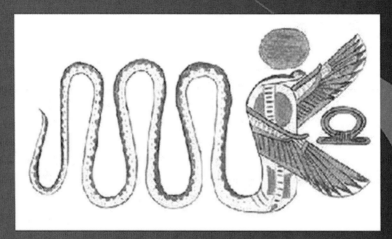

Each day Ra defeated the evil serpent.

Egyptian Mythology

One of the most prominent Egyptian myths was that of the daily battle of the Sun god Ra against Apep, an evil god depicted as a great serpent that was the deification of darkness and chaos. Ra had to do battle against him every morning before he could rise from the East and each day the Sun won the battle.

Babylonian Star Chart - 2084 BC

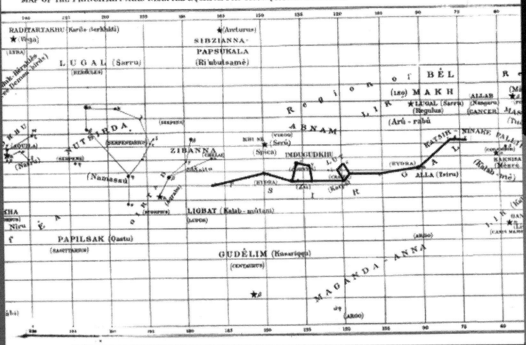

Fig. II. THE BABYLONIAN CELESTIAL SPHERE.
MAP OF THE PRINCIPAL STARS NEAR THE EQUATOR FOR THE EQUINOX B.C. 2084.

The History of the Constellation Hydra

Babylonians called it Tsir-gal. (The Great Snake)   In this Babylonian star chart from 2084 BC, it is shown as a winged serpent, which proves that astronomers illustrated it this way in very ancient times.

Ancient Phoenician Star Chart - 1200 BC

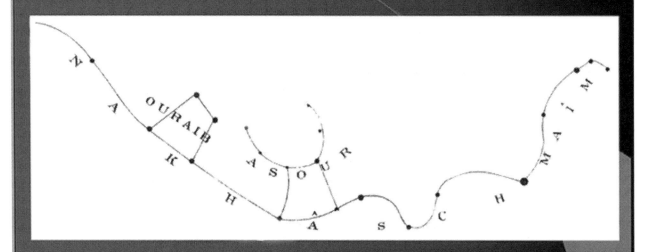

The ancient Phoenicians called it Nakhasch-maim (The Snake, or The Great Snake) in the time of this 1200 B.C. Phoenician star chart.

The Greeks called it Hydra

It was called Hydra (The Water Snake) by the Greeks.

The reason we have Greek names for the star constellations is because the Greeks, with Alexander the Great, conquered Egypt in 332 BC. Once the ruling power was the Greeks, their names for the star constellations replaced those of the Egyptians.

Sextans, Crater, Corvus, and new Hydra

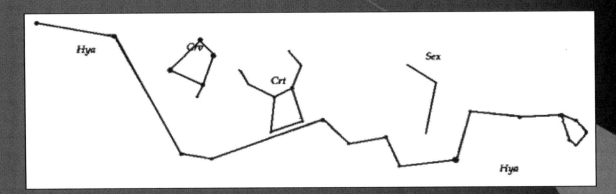

Flamsteed and Hevelius divided the former constellation of Hydra into individual constellations in 17th century

Finally, in the 17th century, stellar cartographers Flamsteed and Hevelius, broke the old Hydra constellation into Sextans (the sextant), Crater (the cup), Corvus (the crow) and a new, reduced Hydra.

Hydra at its apex just before dawn

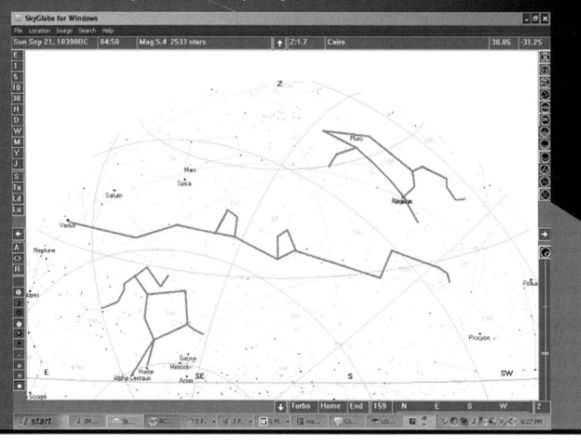

The Battle of the Serpent and the Sun God

If we look at the Egyptian myth of the battle between the Great Serpent and the Sun God in the context of astronomy, we can see that on September 21st 10,390 BC, Hydra reached its highest position in the sky just before dawn, at which time the rays of the sun pierced Hydra and destroyed its visibility. The tomb drawings of snakes being cut with knives were not depicting physical violence at all, but were symbolic of an astronomical event.

This was the reason for the creation of the legend of the battle between the Sun God and the great evil serpent Apep. It was developed to preserve the date of the sealing of the Hall of Records!

Bringing in Astronomy to Assist the Chronology of History

Sir Norman Lockyer

1836-1920

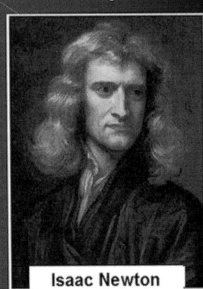

Isaac Newton

1643-1727

Egyptian mythology was intensely astronomical

Mythology and Astronomy

Sir Norman Lockyer (1836-1920) one of the major English astronomers of his time, in 1890 became interested in a problem which had also attracted Isaac Newton, that of bringing in astronomy to assist the chronology of history.

Lockyer derived his conclusions about the astronomical character of Egyptian religion on the solidest architectural measurements and astronomical calculations. As he carried out his research, it soon became obvious to him that their mythology was intensely astronomical. In 1894 he published his study of astronomy and mythology of the ancient Egyptians, *The Dawn of Astronomy.* It is excellent reading if you have not read it.

Lockyer proved that by knowing the position a star rose on the horizon, the date that it rose in that position could be discovered by using astronomy. In the case of the ancient Egyptians, what was needed was our recognition of how they identified Hydra.

Hydra in the tombs of the Valley of the Kings

Tuthmosis III - 1425 BC

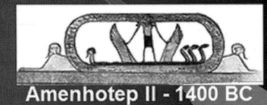

Amenhotep II - 1400 BC

Seti I - 1279 BC

Ramesses VI - 1137 BC

It's easy to imagine that a multi-headed winged serpent might represent a great snake constellation suspended in the night sky. Hydra is the largest of all constellations and was shown as a multi-headed winged serpent in the tombs of the ancient Kings of Egypt for three centuries.

From what has been presented so far, we know that Hydra was portrayed as a great flying snake by many ancient civilizations. But when exactly during 10,390 BC was it visible in Egypt in the predawn sky?

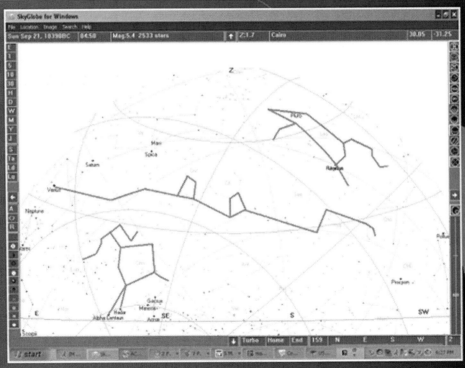

By using our computer program, we regenerated the positions of the stars over Egypt as they appeared in those ancient times. As we scrolled through the months, looking at the predawn sky, it was on September 15th that the position of the constellation Hydra was horizontal in the sky, matching the way it was painted in the tombs of the Valley of the Kings (top image). We discovered that it was also possible to pinpoint the exact day by paying attention to the *head* at the tail of Hydra in the tomb drawing.

The ancient Egyptian astronomers represented planets as gods. The head at the tail of that serpent is the head of a god, suggesting that it represents a planet. With this in mind we considered the positions of the planets in relationship to Hydra during the middle of September 10,390 BC. Our computer program shows that Venus was the only planet in the vicinity to be considered as a candidate. From September 16th until September 25th of that year Venus was in Libra, and the midway point, September 21st, is the Autumnal Equinox, a significant day for astronomers.

First Star of Hydra at 120 degrees 10,390 BC

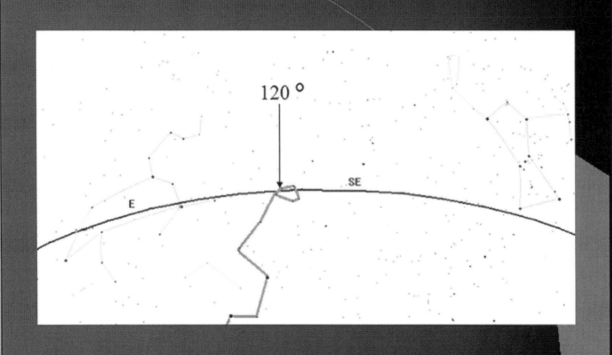

But there's more...

More astronomical proof is to be found within the tombs of the kings, in the Book of Am Tuat. This ancient book gives the position of the first star of Hydra rising at 120 over the gateway of the horizon.

Using the science of astronomy we discovered the date was September 21st, 10,390 BC when this star was in this position as recorded in the ancient Egyptian texts. This year also agrees with the year that Edgar Cayce gave for the completion of Giza and the sealing of the Hall of Records.

The Readings are Hard to Read

Reading 254-63, #4 says:

Q. How can the language used in the readings be made clearer, more concise and more direct?

A. Be able to understand it better!

Why did they make the Readings so Hard to Understand?

Cayce's transcriptions, for various reasons, are often awkward and difficult to understand. Someone who received a reading from Cayce asked if the readings could be made easier to understand. The answer given by Cayce was this: learn to understand them better!

The same advice can be applied to the Egyptian texts. The ancient Egyptians did not look at the world the way we do. They seem to have combined two or more ideas with respect to their concepts of gods, heavenly bodies, and other celestial beings, in a manner that doesn't match the way we look at things today. But perhaps the answer is to learn to understand them better! They were good astronomers. Their knowledge of the stars predates present-day historical estimates of their civilization.

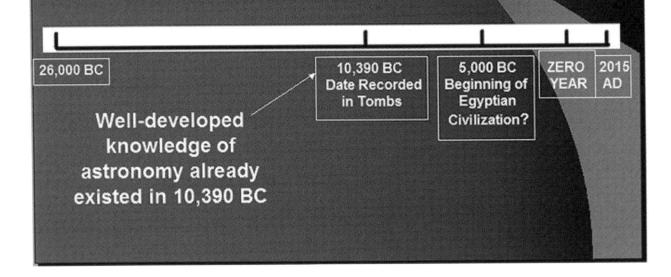

The Egyptian civilization has been estimated to have begun about 5,000 BC. But since the rising of the first star of Hydra on the horizon was recorded as 120 in the tombs of the Kings of Egypt, and since the only time this star ever rose at 120 degrees during the current 26,000-year cycle of precession was on September 21st, 10,390 BC, the implication is that the beginning of Egyptian civilization could be at least 5,000 years older than has been previously estimated. (And if consideration is given for the amount of time necessary for the evolution and development of astronomy, the Egyptian civilization could be much older.)

It is no wonder it takes much study and effort, as well as a willingness to think of the world differently, to be able to fathom the true meanings as they were intended.

The three sphinx guardians identified so far:

1. The Great Sphinx
2. The Constellation Centaurus
3. The Constellation Leo

IS THAT ALL OF THEM?

So far during this presentation we have identified three *sphinx* guardians of the Hall of Records.

1. The Great Sphinx
2. The Constellation of Centaurus
3. The Constellation of Leo

But are there other guardians of the Hall of Records?

The Serpent Guard

950 BC

The Serpent Guardian

There is another guard not specifically mentioned as a guard in the readings, but it is shown in the ancient Egyptian texts.

Above the seated figure of Osiris, the text reads: **Osiris upon his throne**

Written upon the pyramid: **The Throne of Osiris**

This illustration is from an ancient Egyptian papyrus that belonged to a princess of Egypt in 950 BC. It shows a serpent guarding the tomb of Osiris, which is at the top of the pyramid!

Location of Osiris and the Hall of Records

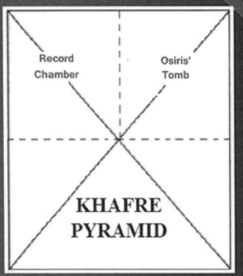

The Cayce readings explain there is a tomb in the Northeast corner of the first pyramid builded, and the Hall of Records is in the Northwest corner of this same pyramid.

> *"In the first of the pyramids built in the Valley of the Shadow, there still may be found unto this day portions of data as was preserved with the ruler, who afterward was worshiped as the representative of God made manifest in earth. These will be found in the northwest corner or chamber of this mound."* (5748-4)

> *"The entity then, in the upper chamber of the northeast corner of the first pyramid builded"* (341-8)

The Tomb of Osiris

Throne of Osiris

Culmination of a star

pyramid

interior

sacred place

tomb

This illustration of a serpent guardian was found on a 21st dynasty coffin discovered in Thebes.

The hieroglyphs show the throne of Osiris and the zenith of the constellation of the serpent above the interior of the sacred place of his tomb.

At the bottom of this slide we show the individual symbols and what they mean, so that you can see how this image was designed to convey the location of the tomb of Osiris.

Serpent Guardian of Osiris

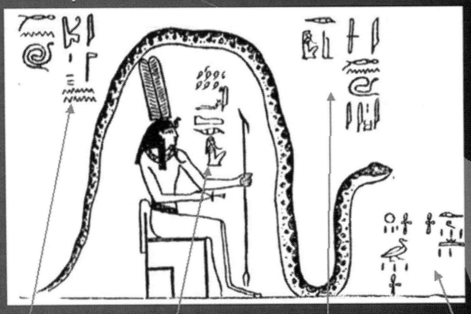

Hail God this in serpent's embrace

Dead body of Osiris

Osiris who is in embrace of Apep

Serpent guardian of the body of Osiris

The Serpent Guardian of Osiris from the Seventh Division of Am Tuat

Written above Osiris on his throne:
The dead body of Osiris

Written behind the serpent:
Hail this god in the serpent's embrace

Written above the head of the serpent:
Osiris who is in the embrace of Apep

Written in front of the serpent:

The serpent guardian of the body of Osiris.

*Clearly, the Egyptians are telling us that
this is the serpent guardian of the tomb of Osiris!*

The Guards of the Hall of Records

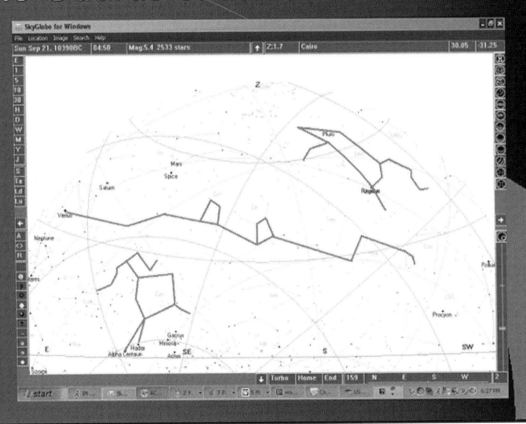

**These are the Guards
of the Hall of Records**

The Vastness of Time

The Prague Astronomical Clock

The Vastness of Time

Once we begin to study history from an astronomical perspective, our scale of measurement expands exponentially because of the vastness of time involved in measuring celestial changes. This shift of reference in time exists within the readings, where we find allusions to terrestrial time and to zodiac time.

Reading for Miss 993

Reading for Miss 993

For example, few people who have studied the Cayce material realize the time scale discussed within the readings given for a woman identified only as Miss 993. One of her readings explains that the date for the construction of the first of the pyramids at Gizeh was in the neighborhood of 250,000 BC, which equates to somewhere between nine and ten cycles of precession (a cycle of procession is about 26,000 years).

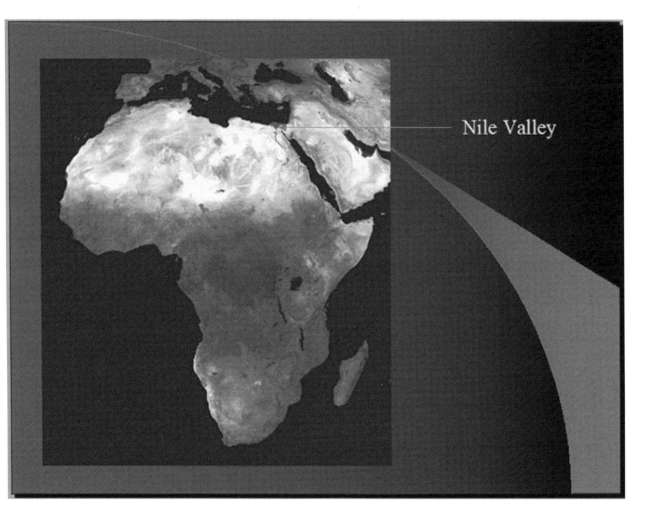

Nile Valley

The readings explain that Gizeh had been submerged for nearly a quarter of a million years since civilization had been in that part of the continent.

From Cayce's readings, we learn that a nomadic group of people entered into Egypt in the eleventh millennium BC and through archeological research discovered the remains of monuments and structures created by an unknown, previous civilization that had flourished there long before their arrival. After this wandering tribe had settled down into the Nile Valley, the readings explain that they unearthed monuments from time to time, and added to them. Some of which are still existent.

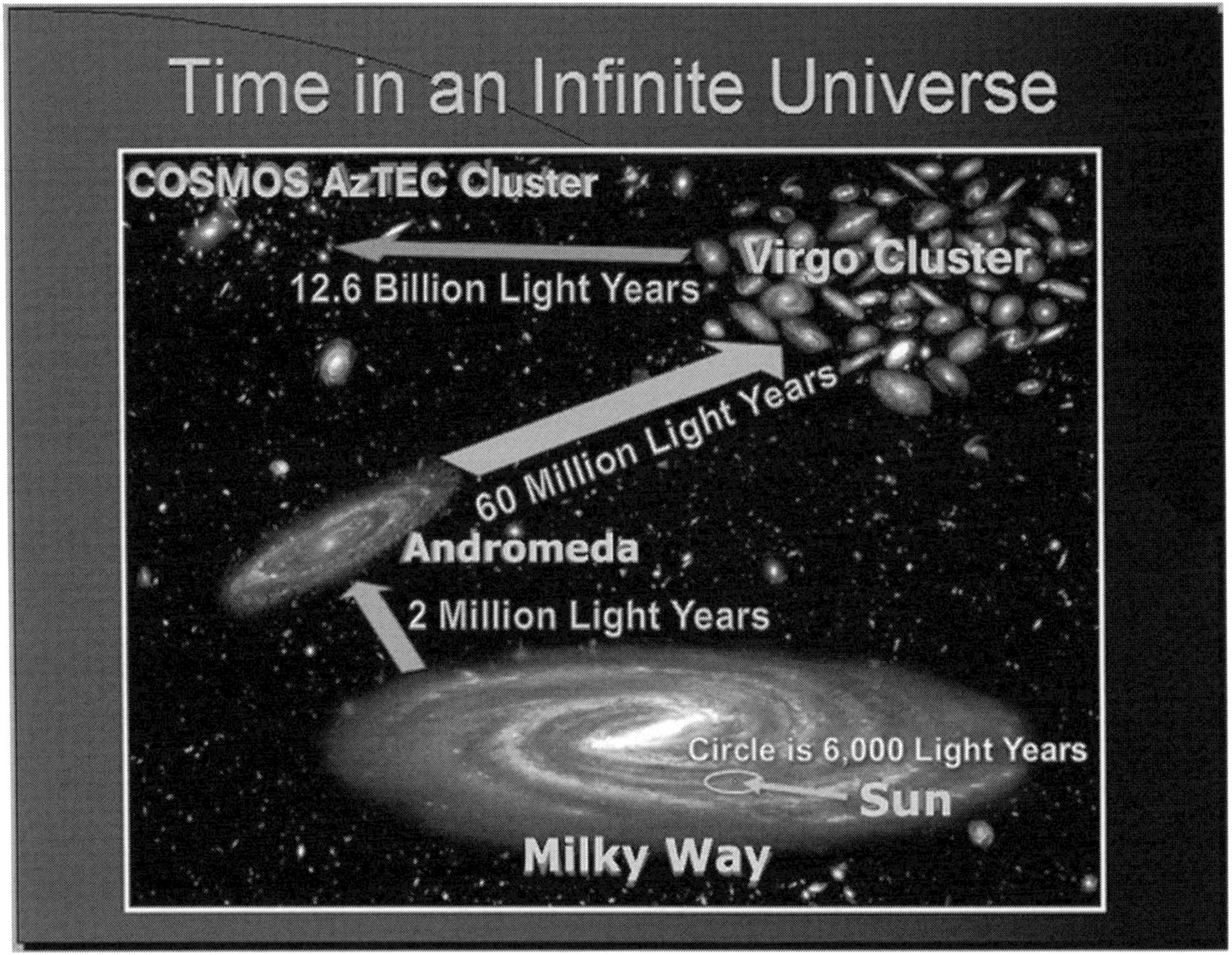
Time in an Infinite Universe
COSMOS AzTEC Cluster
12.6 Billion Light Years
Virgo Cluster
60 Million Light Years
Andromeda
2 Million Light Years
Circle is 6,000 Light Years
Sun
Milky Way

From an astronomical perspective in the scheme of an infinite universe, a quarter of a million years is not long at all. But from the position of historical orientation on Earth, it seems quite outside the realm of realistic possibility that a civilization existed in Egypt that long ago.

MICHAEL A. HOFFMAN

EGYPT
BEFORE
THE
PHARAOHS

The story of the great
archaeological discoveries
over the last 85 years
that have given us our first
coherent picture of the
life and culture of prehistoric
Egypt—told by a participant
in the most recent excavations

However, recent archeological discoveries have brought to light the existence of a prehistoric culture in Egypt nearly a million years ago. This information can be found in Michael Hoffman's book *Egypt before the Pharaohs.*

Temple at Edfu

The Temple at Edfu

Turning our attention to a historical account of early Egypt, we find documents inscribed upon the walls of an ancient Egyptian temple located on the west bank of the Nile, in the city of Edfu. These inscriptions provide information on the myths and religion of ancient Egypt.

The Serpent in the Sky

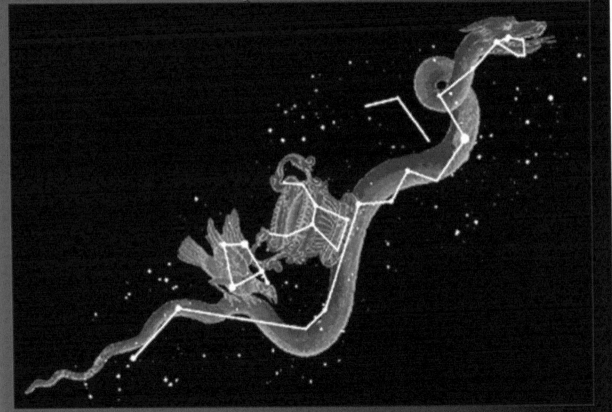

The text is very obscure in parts but there is allusion
to a fight against a snake that took place in the sky.

Primeval Ones

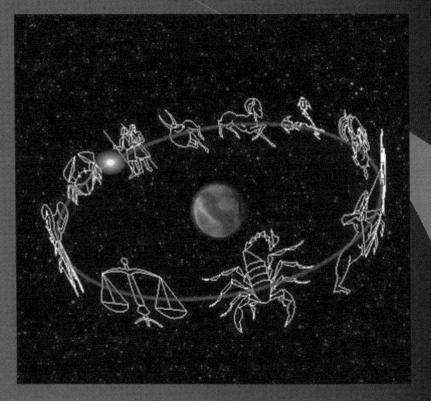

Other references are to the Primeval Ones. The general definition
of their nature was that they existed before everything else. They
shaped their own bodily appearance and they were radiant. The
appearance of these divine beings resembled animals such as
falcons, lions, snakes, and bulls. There is no doubt that these were
star constellations.

The Age of Taurus the Bull

TAURUS

By using our computer star program, we have learned that the year 10,390 BC was in the zodiac age of the Taurus the Bull. This may indicate the date to which these ancient records were referring, because the first mention of the appearance of these Primeval Ones in the Edfu text indicates that they resembled Bulls.

Ruins of a Former Civilization

The texts of Edfu also explain that after the death of the first sacred, mythical world, new inhabitants came into the region and discovered the ruins of a former civilization and they rebuilt it.

"There was even then the seeking through those channels that today are called archaeological research ... when there was the entrance of Araart and Araaraart, they began to build upon the mounds they discovered through research."

Once again the Edgar Cayce material is in agreement with historical documents of ancient Egypt.

Cayce said, *"There was even then the seeking through those channels that today are called archaeological research...when there was the entrance of Araart and Araaraart, they began to build upon the mounds they discovered through research."*

Mark Lehner notes the difference in construction styles in the Khafre Pyramid, indicating 2 different time periods may be involved.

From this ... to this

In his book titled *The Complete Pyramids*, Mark Lehner, former ARE member, explained that the pyramid of Khafre was built in two separate sections. Professor Lehner indicated that the top of the pyramid was of a different construction style than the lower base and he suggests this might be because there was a stop in the construction and then later a resumption of building.[3]

---

[3] Lehner, Mark. 1997. *The complete pyramids*. New York: Thames and Hudson, page 122.

Edgar Cayce
Readings

Egyptian
Texts

Astronomy

The information that has been presented here is from Edgar Cayce's readings, ancient Egyptian texts, and astronomy. These three places, when taken together, indicate that the location of the Hall of Records is not under the Sphinx, but at the top of the middle pyramid on the Gizeh plateau in Egypt.

THE LOCATION OF THE HALL OF RECORDS

It seems that we need to put more effort into trying to understand Cayce in a broader context. There are difficulties in dealing with the Cayce readings, and even well researched ideas, like this one, might turn out to be wrong. Let's not forget how easy it was to assume that the Hall of Records was located in an underground corridor proceeding from the paw of the Sphinx!

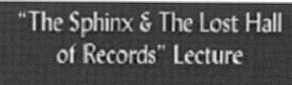

"The Sphinx & The Lost Hall of Records" Lecture

John Bunker
and Karen Pressler

Edgar Cayce's A.R.E. Houston Center

Other Titles by Bunker Pressler Books

*Edgar Cayce and
The Urantia Book*

by John M. Bunker
and Karen L. Pressler

ISBN 978-0966977417

The Book of Aker

by John M. Bunker
and Karen L. Pressler

ISBN 978-0966977431

*A Sailor
and his Ship:
The Voyage of the
USS Shoshone
(AKA-65)*

by D.D. Cayce

ISBN 978-0988500129

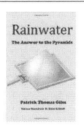

*Rainwater: The
Answer to the
Pyramids*

By Patrick Giles

ISBN 978-0966977448

The Am Tuat

By Paul Bucher

ISBN 978-0988500150

*The Story of Zoo-Key-
Knee and the Origin of
Rute-of Bagas*

By John Bunker

ISBN 978-0966977493

And newest release:

Edgar Cayce and the Hall of Records

**By John M. Bunker
and Karen L. Pressler**

ISBN   978-0966977486

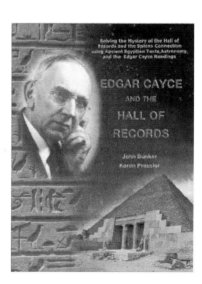

29996674R00105

Made in the USA
San Bernardino, CA
03 February 2016